LIFE-CHANGING SALAD DRESSINGS IN 3 MINUTES FLAT

TABLE OF CONTENTS

Dressing makes the salad—you know it's true. Dressings turn bland, ordinary (but nutritious) vegetables and leafy greens into lip-smacking goodness. Dressings also give salads and fruits a distinctive personality, and a nod to a certain culture or region of the world. In these pages you'll find delicious dressings for every occasion, many of which can also serve as wonderful marinades, dipping sauces, and sandwich slathers.

Like most people these days, you probably have little time for long, confusing recipes. Bottled, store-bought dressings are convenient but don't taste half as good as these fresh ones. And with simple prep techniques and some pantry organization, these go together in a flash. You might not even need the full three minutes and, if you're like me, will never buy a bottled dressing again.

The dressings in this book are either creamy or vinaigrette style with very few exceptions. *Vinaigrette* is essentially the combination of any oil and acid mixed together, complimented with the addition of other flavors such as herbs, spices, a sweetening agent for balance, and any number of prepared condiments. The recipes are gluten free and vegetarian (unless you count anchovies as a meat!) and can all be chilled for storage in the refrigerator for a week or more depending on the delicacy of the fresh herbs used.

The main thing to remember is that the quality of your finished product will depend completely upon the quality of your ingredients. Don't skimp on quality. Now dig in and find a flavor combination that makes *your* mouth water. Your family and friends will undoubtedly love it too.

~Grace Légere

A Stocked Pantry Equals Fast Dressings

About oils

These days there are many different oils to choose from and each will bring a different influence to your finished salad dressing. Have several different oils on hand in your pantry so that you always have just the right one. Olive oils can be heavy-tasting and come in a range from bitter to fruity. Other types of oils are essentially tasteless and serve only as a binder for the other flavorings and ingredients. Lighter oils will make a lighter dressing.

In each recipe you'll see what I prefer, but in a pinch any oil will do. These may include Extra Virgin olive oil, regular olive oil, light olive oil, canola oil, peanut oil, corn oil, sunflower oil, and vegetable oil.

About vinegars

The type of vinegar you use in a salad dressing will *greatly* impact the flavor profile so try to use the one I specify in my recipes. In general, never use white distilled vinegar. Save it for cleaning your windows.

Try to learn which vinegars are sourer than others. Learn which ones you and your loved ones enjoy most. These may include red wine vinegar, white wine vinegar, sherry vinegar, balsamic vinegar, apple cider vinegar, rice wine vinegar, and even gourmet flavored vinegars.

About citrus

When the recipe features citrus flavors, freshly squeezed juice will often act as the acid component instead of vinegar. Invest in a cook's rasp for quick, easy zesting of the fruit's flavorful outer skin, and always refrigerate these types of dressing to keep them fresh.

About spices and seasonings

Dried, bottled herbs and spices should be replaced every year for freshness. Use sparingly as they are potent. The following recipes call mostly for fresh herbs so have them cleaned, stemmed, chopped, and ready before you begin preparing the dressing.

About fresh herbs

Always refrigerate fresh herbs except in the case of basil, which prefers to be out on the countertop in a glass of water –like flowers in a vase. To chop the leaves of fresh thyme, rosemary, oregano, you must de-stem them first... they will release their leaves more readily if you gently pull them backwards from the stem with two fingers.

About aromatics

Flavor-makers such as garlic, shallot, ginger, and onion should be stored in a cool, dry place and used within a week or so of purchasing. Never use one that has gone soft or is showing signs of mold. Aromatics should be firm and fragrant, and minced up within a short time of being used in the recipe.

Emulsifiers

Mustards, mayonnaise, honey, and certain cheeses will literally bring your dressing "together" while adding great flavor and texture. A small whisk is all you should need to produce a well blended dressing.

Some Useful Tips

The proportions used here will make a robust dressing, usually a half-cup oil to 3 T. vinegar or citrus juice, but feel free to vary this to your own taste in regard to the sharpness desired.

These recipes contain exact measurements but can also be "estimated" in the glass bowl, especially as you become more experienced at making homemade dressings. Most will yield enough dressing for a large salad feeding four to six people, or a smaller *side* salad for eight to twelve people. If you want less simply half it, or for more double it. Remember, you can always store any extra for use at another time.

Items you'll need include a small glass or metal bowl approximately 6" to 8" in diameter, a mini whisk, a set of measuring spoons, a measuring cup, a cook's rasp for proper zesting of fresh citrus skin, a small seed-catching citrus juicer, and some plastic wrap. *(Prior ingredient preparation may require a chef's knife, cutting board, zester, grater, and a colander depending on the fresh ingredients used.)*

How to store: Dressings can be saved right in their glass mixing bowl with plastic wrap pulled tightly over the top, or poured into a clean (sterile) jar or plastic storage container. When storing dressings containing fresh herbs, citrus, or fruit components, always refrigerate!

To salt or not to salt? If you're observing a low salt diet, feel free to half the amount shown or leave it out completely. I recommend using coarse or kosher salt whenever salt is called for.

Prepare all ingredients beforehand. Our super-fast, three minute timeframe assumes your fresh herbs, citrus, aromatics, and other flavorings are already washed and prepared! Dried herbs are stronger than their fresh counterparts so remember to use less if substituting. (Oregano and tarragon are the only two dried herbs I would ever consider using in dressings.) When fresh citrus is called for, be sure to zest the outer skin *before* cutting the fruit in half.

A note on food safety: Always use sterilized jars or clean plastic containers for storage if you're making more than you intend to use. Always keep mayonnaise and mayonnaise-based dressing properly chilled in a refrigerator. Dressings with ingredients like fresh herbs or fruits will keep for a week in the refrigerator. Spices should have a relatively recent shelf life so that they're fresh-tasting and free of any critters.

Taste it! Dressings made at home can be flexible to the preferences and palates of those who will be enjoying it. Don't be afraid to taste your dressing with a clean spoon...this is the only way you'll know if it is salty enough, sweet enough, or vinegary enough for you and your loved ones. My recipes are merely a guideline...adjust accordingly.

How to make homemade mayonnaise

Yes, you read correctly... homemade mayonnaise is easy to make and is arguably better when it's made with pure ingredients from your kitchen. It's more economical too!

1 whole egg, plus one yolk
2 t. fresh lemon juice (or apple cider vinegar)
¼ t. kosher salt, to taste
1½ t. dry mustard powder
1½ t. white granulated sugar
1 c. canola oil (or avocado oil)

(Should be prepared in a food processor or blender)
    Combine the egg and extra yolk, lemon juice or vinegar, a splash of the oil, salt, sugar and the dry mustard and blend for about two minutes. Scrape sides to insure proper mixing of ingredients. Place lid over container and restart the blades...while it's beating, slowly add the remaining oil and blend until it becomes thick and, well... mayonnaise-like. Delicious! *Yields one cup*

Know my cooking abbreviations

t.   means *teaspoon*
T.   means *tablespoon*
c.   means *cup*
oz.   means *fluid ounces*
lbs.   means *pounds*

French Vinaigrettes

Ah, the French! Culinary masters for centuries to be sure, and claimants of the original *Vinaigrette*. In these classic combinations, favorite French flavors prevail.

- **The simple instructions:**
In a small bowl, blend all ingredients together with a small whisk. Some will emulsify more than others, which is normal. To store, simply cover and chill.

The Original Vinaigrette
Classically French, and simply perfect on mixed baby greens

½ c. extra virgin olive oil
3 T. sherry vinegar
1 t. real Dijon mustard
1 T. finely chopped fresh shallot
Pinch of salt, to taste
Pinch of ground pepper, to taste

French Dijon Vinaigrette
With an emphasis on mustard and garlic, the piquant flavors bring sophistication

½ c. extra virgin olive oil
3 T. red wine vinegar
1 t. Dijon mustard
1 clove minced fresh garlic
Pinch of salt, to taste
Pinch of ground pepper, to taste

Celery Seed Vinaigrette
Try this on tender, cooked baby potatoes and greens for a very special salad

½ c. extra virgin olive oil
3 T. white wine vinegar
1 t. celery seeds
1 t. sugar
1 t. prepared mustard
Pinch of salt, to taste
Pinch of ground pepper, to taste

Shallot, Mustard & Capers Vinaigrette
The agreeable sharpness of these ingredients makes for a sophisticated blend

½ c. extra virgin olive oil
3 T. red wine vinegar
2 t. minced fresh shallot
1 t. jarred capers, drained of their brine
1 t. Dijon mustard
Pinch of salt, to taste
Pinch of ground pepper, to taste

Champagne Vinaigrette
Champagne vinegar is a bit of a splurge but creates a lovely, light vinaigrette

½ c. light olive oil
3 T. champagne vinegar
1 T. honey
1 T. chopped fresh parsley
Pinch of salt and freshly ground pepper, to taste

Italian Vinaigrettes

Italians would never ever serve a creamy salad dressing and so these will again be *vinaigrette* style dressings. The particular herbs, cheese, and sometimes garlic, give these combinations a decidedly Italian taste.

- **The simple instructions:**
In a small bowl, blend all ingredients together with a small whisk. Some will emulsify more than others, which is normal. To store, simply cover and chill.

Classic Italian
The purest, simplest one of all

½ c. extra virgin olive oil
3 T. red wine vinegar
Pinch of salt, to taste
Pinch of ground pepper, to taste
(Even with a whisk these ingredients will not emulsify, so just
blend them the best you can and then use immediately.)

Balsamic Vinaigrette
*This is the favorite in our home - I can make it in less
than a minute*

½ c. extra virgin olive oil
3 T. aged balsamic vinegar
½ t. dried oregano (or 1 t. chopped fresh oregano)
1 T. honey
1 t. prepared mustard
Pinch of salt, to taste
Pinch of ground pepper, to taste

Red Wine Vinaigrette
Sweet and sour in nature, this dressing perks up any salad

½ c. extra virgin olive oil
3 T. red wine vinegar
1 t. prepared mustard
1 T. sugar
1 clove fresh garlic, chopped
1 T. minced fresh shallot
Pinch of salt, to taste
Pinch of ground pepper, to taste

Caprino Vinaigrette
Goat cheese adds a unique and irresistible earthy quality to this dressing

½ c. extra virgin olive oil
3 T. white wine vinegar
1 T. soft goat cheese
1 t. honey
Pinch of ground pepper and a little salt, to taste

Double Olive Vinaigrette
Chopped green olives add an extra punch to this olive oil-based dressing

½ c. extra virgin olive oil
3 T. white wine vinegar
1 T. chopped marinated green olives (like Spanish Manzanilla olives)
2 t. chopped fresh parsley
1 t. sugar
1 T. finely grated Parmesan cheese
Pinch of ground pepper, to taste

Anchovy Herb Vinaigrette
Salty and tangy, this delicious dressing may change the way you feel about those little hairy fishes

½ c. extra virgin olive oil
3 T. red wine vinegar
1 t. good quality, jarred anchovy paste
1 t. jarred capers, drained of their brine
1 t. minced fresh shallot
2 t. chopped fresh parsley
Pinch of salt, to taste
Pinch of ground pepper, to taste

Sicilian Cupboard Dressing
The only dressing any respectable Sicilian Grandma would ever serve!

After blending, pour into a jar or capped bottle and store in a cupboard at room temperature for use whenever needed. (If using a narrow necked bottle, just push the smashed garlic one by one into it by hand.) The following recipe makes a hefty quantity.

1½ c. extra virgin olive oil
9 T. red wine vinegar (½ c. plus 1 T.)
1-2 large smashed cloves of fresh garlic, to taste
1 T. dried oregano
1 ½ T. granulated sugar, or less to taste
Pinch of salt, to taste
Pinch of ground pepper, to taste

American Classic Dressings

These traditional American favorites come in both creamy and vinaigrette styles and taste so much better when you make them up fresh at home. All are suitable on just about any vegetable salad you can think up, or as a dipping sauce.

- **The simple instructions:** In a small bowl, blend all ingredients together with a small whisk. Some will emulsify more than others, which is normal. To store, simply cover and chill.

Creamy Blue Cheese Dressing
This tangy dressing is super-famous for a reason

½ c. mayonnaise
¼ c. milk
¼ c. sour cream
1 t. Worcestershire sauce
¼ c. to ½ c. blue cheese (depending on its pungency) crumbled up
Pinch of salt and pepper, to taste

Spicy Russian Dressing
The delicious, hot flavor of horseradish makes this famous dressing a real standout

½ c. mayonnaise
1 t. white wine vinegar
1 t. plain, prepared horseradish - to taste
2 T. ketchup or chili sauce
2 t. minced fresh shallot or onion
¼ t. ground paprika
1 t. Worcestershire sauce
Pinch of salt and pepper, to taste

Thousand Island Dressing
Named for a large river area bordering Canada and New York State, this one looks like Russian dressing but tastes very different from it

½ c. mayonnaise
1½ T. ketchup
4 t. sweet pickle relish
2 t. apple cider vinegar
1 t. sugar
2 T. light oil, like canola, or a bit more if it seems too thick
1/8 t. dry mustard powder
1/8 t. garlic powder
1/8 t. onion powder
Pinch of salt and pepper, to taste

Catalina Dressing
Red, sweet, and sour all at the same time, this dressing was a favorite in the 1960's

½ c. canola oil, or other light-tasting oil
¼ c. ketchup
¼ c. red wine vinegar
1/3 c. sugar
1 t. paprika
½ t. celery seeds
½ t. onion powder
¼ t. garlic powder
¼ t. dried oregano
Pinch of salt and pepper, to taste

American French Dressing
I know it's confusing, but this is the classic red dressing that Americans call French!

½ c. mayonnaise
1 T. ketchup
2 T. light olive oil
1 T. apple cider vinegar
½ t. Worcestershire sauce
½ t. powder garlic
1 t. sugar
1 t. paprika
¼ t. salt
Pinch of freshly ground black pepper

Real Caesar Dressing
Whisked up with raw egg yolk for richness, this dressing is not recommended for children, the elderly, or un-healthy individuals

4 cloves fresh garlic minced into a paste
1 egg yolk (the egg white will not be used)
1 T. fresh lemon juice
1 T. red wine vinegar
1 t. Dijon mustard
1 t. Worcestershire sauce
1 t. anchovy paste
½ c. light olive oil (added last, little by little, as you whisk everything together)
1/8 t. freshly ground black pepper
Pinch of salt if needed, to taste

Homemade Ranch-style Dressing
Your own kitchen ingredients make a knock-out Ranch dressing, which only gets better after it sits for a bit in the fridge

½ c. mayonnaise
¼ c. buttermilk
1 T. apple cider vinegar
1 clove chopped fresh garlic
1 t. chopped chives
1 T. chopped parsley
1 T. chopped dill
½ t. paprika
¼ t. mustard powder
½ t. onion powder
½ t. sugar
Pinch of salt and pepper, to taste

Green Goddess-style Dressing
For a greener color, simply mix this one up in an electric blender

½ c. mayonnaise
1 T. light olive oil
1 t. white wine vinegar
2 t. chopped fresh chives
2 T. chopped fresh parsley
1 large clove chopped fresh garlic
2 T. good quality anchovy paste
1 t. Worcestershire sauce
Pinch of salt and pepper, to taste

Creamy Horseradish Dressing

Spicy hot but oh, so creamy... try this one on a steak salad

½ c. mayonnaise
½ c. heavy cream
½ c. prepared horseradish sauce
1 T. sugar
2 t. Dijon mustard
Pinch of salt and pepper, to taste

Asian Dressings & Dipping Sauce

Looking for something more exotic to dress up a Chinese Chicken Salad or Asian Veggie Salad? Here are some very tasty dressings that will take your taste buds for a walk through the Asian Continent. I have also included a professional restaurant-style dipping sauce which can be served alongside pot-stickers and dumplings.

- **The simple instructions:**

In a small bowl, blend all ingredients together with a small whisk. Some will emulsify more than others, which is normal. To store, simply cover and chill.

Asian Inspired Salad Dressing
Perfect on your homemade Chinese chicken salad

½ c. light tasting oil, like canola or peanut
3 T. rice wine vinegar *(plain or seasoned)*
1 T. sesame oil
1 fresh scallion, chopped on the bias into small pieces
1 t. honey, to taste
1 t. toasted sesame seeds
Pinch of salt, to taste
Pinch of pepper, to taste

Rice Wine Vinaigrette with Fresh Ginger
Fresh ginger adds zip to this lovely dressing

½ c. light tasting oil, like canola or peanut
3 T. rice wine vinegar *(plain or seasoned)*
1 T. sesame oil
1 fresh scallion, chopped on the bias into small pieces
1 one-inch knob of fresh ginger flesh, grated or finely chopped
– its skin can be easily scraped off with a spoon
1 T. honey, to taste
Pinch of salt and pepper, to taste

Japanese Miso Dressing
The savory umami flavor of miso makes this a delicious alternative

3 T. miso paste
2 T. peanut oil
2 T. sesame oil
2 T. seasoned rice wine vinegar
1 t. soy sauce
1 T. fresh lime juice
1 half-inch knob of fresh ginger flesh, grated or finely chopped
    – its skin can be easily scraped off with a spoon
1-2 cloves minced fresh garlic, to taste
2 T. plain yogurt (optional, for creaminess)
2 t. sugar
Small pinch of cayenne pepper

Sweet Thai Style Dipping Sauce
For curry puffs, Thai spring rolls, and Thai-style cole slaw

1 ½ T. sugar
1 T. water
2 T. rice wine vinegar
1 T. fresh squeezed lime juice
1 small clove fresh garlic, chopped
1 T. finely chopped carrot
1 T. finely chopped fresh cucumber
1 t. finely chopped fresh red onion
2 t. good quality fish sauce *(optional)*
Pinch of salt, to taste, *especially if you're skipping the fish sauce*

Pot-stickers Dipping Sauce

If you order Chinese dumplings so that you can get your tastebuds on that garlicky, gingery soy sauce that comes on the side, this is for you. With this easy dipping sauce whisked up in your dressing-making bowl, you'll be able to fully enjoy pot-stickers fried at home.

¼ c. sesame oil

2 T. rice wine vinegar *(plain, not seasoned)*

½ c. soy sauce

2 t. molasses syrup (honey can be substituted but will not taste as authentic)

1 to 2 cloves fresh garlic, to taste

1 one-inch knob grated or finely minced fresh ginger flesh – *its skin can be easily scraped off with a spoon*

Pinch of dried red pepper flakes, to taste

1 fresh scallion, chopped on the bias into small pieces

Memorable
Specialty Dressings

These are my most unique dressing recipes and are simply divine. The final one is my personal favorite so I hope you'll give it a try.

- **The simple instructions:**
In a small bowl, blend all ingredients together with a small whisk. Some will emulsify more than others, which is normal. To store, simply cover and chill.

Hawaiian Sweet and Sour Dressing

A touch of pineapple juice brings this tangy dressing to a higher lever

½ c. light tasting oil, like canola
¼ c. pineapple juice
2 T. fresh lime juice
1 half-inch knob of fresh ginger flesh, grated or finely chopped
– its skin can be easily scraped off with a spoon
1 T. sugar or honey
Pinch of salt, to taste
Pinch of ground pepper

Creamy Gorgonzola Dressing

This recipe offers an Italian version of the famous blue cheese dressing

½ c. mayonnaise
¼ c. milk
¼ c. sour cream
1 t. Worcestershire sauce
¼ c. to ½ c. sweet Gorgonzola cheese (depending on its pungency) crumbled up
Pinch of salt and pepper, to taste

Creamy Goat Cheese Dressing
Rich and creamy Chèvre on a veggie salad means lip-smacking goodness for you

½ c. mayonnaise
¼ c. milk
¼ c. sour cream
1 t. Worcestershire sauce
¼ c. to ½ c. soft goat cheese (depending on its pungency)
crumbled up
Pinch of salt, to taste
Pinch of ground pepper, to taste

The Classic Greek
The combo of vinegar and lemon tastes great on a Greek salad with olives and feta

1/2 c. extra virgin olive oil
2 T. red wine vinegar
1 T. fresh lemon juice
2 cloves minced fresh garlic
1 T. fresh or dried oregano
1 t. sugar
Pinch of salt, to taste
Pinch of pepper, to taste

Tex-Mex Vinaigrette
This is the perfect dressing for a homemade taco salad

½ c. light olive oil
3 T. red wine vinegar or fresh lime juice
1 t. prepared mustard
1 t. ground cumin
1 t. paprika
Pinch of red pepper flakes, to taste
1 t. sugar
Pinch of salt, to taste

Creamy Honey Mustard with Fresh Herbs
An indescribable flavor combination awaits you

Okay, I fully admit this one takes a bit longer than three minutes to prepare but it's definitely worth the time. It's my very favorite salad dressing. I usually double the batch so I can have it at-the-ready for awhile. The recipe below is quite generous so be sure to store any extra in the refrigerator. It's even fabulous as a dipping sauce for vegetable crudités.

1¼ c. mayonnaise (good quality only)
¾ c. vegetable or canola oil (or a touch more if it seems too thick)
3 to 4 T. honey, to taste
¼ c. yellow prepared mustard
3 T. fresh lemon juice
1 t. celery seed
¼ t. curry powder (this *makes* the dressing)
¼ t. dry mustard powder
¼ c. chopped fresh parsley
2 fresh scallions, chopped into small pieces
Pinch of salt and ground pepper, to taste

Dressing Up Fruit

Fruit salads call for a different flavor profile than veggies and greens. The ones here will enhance any fruit you can throw at it. The first four will add tang and balance; the last one will add sweetness.

- **The simple instructions:**
In a small bowl, blend all ingredients together with a small whisk. Some will emulsify more than others, which is normal. To store, simply cover and chill. Dressings with ingredients like fresh herbs or fruits will keep for a week in the refrigerator, *(excluding the whipped cream preparation below.)*

Lemon Honey Vinaigrette
Great on fruit, but for a delicious salad try this dressing on a bed of arugula and chopped, toasted hazelnuts

½ c. light tasting oil, like grapeseed or canola
3 T. fresh lemon juice
2 T. honey
Pinch of salt and pepper, to taste

Raspberry Vinaigrette
Fresh raspberries and ground walnuts make this a special dressing on greens as well as fruit

½ c. light tasting oil, like grapeseed or walnut oil
1 T. fresh lemon juice
2 T. raspberry-infused vinegar
¼ c. crushed fresh raspberries and their juice
1 T. finely chopped or ground walnuts or almonds
1 T. sugar or honey
Salt and ground pepper, if desired

Poppy Seed Dressing
Probably the most unusual dressing in the world, this one is very easy to make

1/2 c. light tasting oil, like grapeseed or canola
1/3 c. apple cider vinegar
1/3 c. honey
1 t. Dijon mustard
1½ T. poppy seeds
Pinch of salt, to taste

Citrus Dressing

Oranges, lemons, & limes come together in a very piquant dressing

½ c. light tasting oil, like grapeseed or canola
2 t. grated fresh orange zest
1 T. fresh lemon juice
1 T. fresh lime juice
1 T. fresh orange juice
2 T. honey
Pinch of salt, to taste

Chantilly Whipped Cream

Preparation is more than 3 minutes due to the process of whipping the cream. It does not keep long, even in the fridge, so use immediately

2 c. cold heavy cream (or whipping cream)
½ c. confectioner's sugar
1 T. real vanilla extract, to taste

Beat ingredients together with an electric mixer until light and fluffy and holding its peaks. Be careful not to over beat or you'll end up with homemade butter! (If you do, simply order my amazing book *Life-changing Compound Butters In 3 Minutes Flat*.) Enjoy!

Calling all cooks!

Thank you so much for your interest in my recipes. It was great fun bringing you these wonderful flavor combinations...

Please note that the star rating available to you as a customer of this book is for *metadata use only* and <u>does not actually affect this book's viewable online rating!</u> If you enjoyed *Life-changing Salad Dressings*, please take a moment to leave a short customer review on Amazon so that your rating will count for us. Even a few sentences would be helpful, and greatly appreciated.

~*Grace*

Books by Grace Légere

Life-Changing Compound Butters In 3 Minutes Flat

Life-Changing Salad Dressings In 3 Minutes Flat

Life-Changing Potato Salads In 30 Minutes Flat

Life-Changing Salsa Fresca In 30 Minutes Or Less

Cover art created by Dean Dalton

40070710R00029

Made in the USA
San Bernardino, CA
23 June 2019